Cloud 9-1 GCSE REVISION NOTES FOR WILLY RUSSELL'S *BLOOD BROTHERS*

Study Guide Part 6 (with AQA-style sample assessment questions and notes)

by Joe Broadfoot MA

ISBN-13:
978-1973814702

ISBN-10:
1973814706

DEDICATION

To all GCSE students, who want to be on 'cloud nine' come results day!
Cloud 9-1 is here to help you move from grade 1 or above to 9.

CONTENTS

ACKNOWLEDGMENTS

A big thank you to those who have supported in me in my career and also thanks to those that haven't, as your negativity changes to something more positive.

AQA-style Specimen Assessment Material 16: Blood Brothers

How does Russell present the Mickey in *Blood Brothers*?

Write about:
• what Mickey says and does in the play
• how Russell presents Mickey by the way he writes.

PLEASE NOTE, THERE ARE NO EXTRACTS FOR THE MODERN TEXTS SECTION, BUT THE FOLLOWING EXTRACT IS BELOW FOR GUIDANCE TO HELP YOU TO FORM AN ANSWER.

At this point in the play, Mickey has just been scolded by Mrs Johnstone for 'playin' with those hooligans down at the rough end' of the street. Mickey has been told to 'outside the front door' when his mother can see him. This extract is important because the audience can learn about Mickey's character through his soliloquy.

EXTRACT

Mickey *sits, bored, looking at the ants on the pavement.*

Mickey: *(reciting)* I wish I was our Sammy
    Our Sammy's nearly ten.
    He's got two worms and a catapult
    An' he's built a underground den.
    But I'm not allowed to go in there,
    I have to stay near the gate,
    'Cos me Mam says I'm only seven,
    But I'm not, I'm nearly eight!
    I sometimes hate our Sammy,
    He robbed me toy car y' know,
    Now the wheels are missin' an' the top's
broke off,
    An' the bleedin' thing won't go.
    An' he said when he took it, it was just
like that,
    But it wasn't, it went dead straight,
    But y' can't say nott'n when they think y'
seven
    An' y' not, y' nearly eight.
    I wish I was our Sammy,
    Y' wanna see him spit,
    Straight in y' eye from twenty yards

Comment [JB(|: AO2 – 'Ants' could connote insignificance, which foreshadows the negligible impact that Mickey will make on the world during his

Comment [JB(|: AO2 – This is an interesting stage direction, as it is very rare that actors are told to sound like they are 'reciting'. Somehow, the actor has to

Comment [JB(|: AO1 – Mickey's wishful thinking tells us already about how he is discontented with life.
AO2 – Mickey does not use the past

Comment [JB(|: AO2 – The informality of 'our Sammy' is characteristic of the Liverpudlian or Scouse dialect. By using this phrase, Mickey is identifying himself

Comment [JB(|: AO1 – Mickey's admiration for Sammy and his weaponry is made clear at the start of the soliloquy.
AO2 – The semantic field of weaponry

Comment [JB(|: AO3 – In the 1950s and 1960s, an underworld empire of protection rackets, violence and

Comment [JB(|: AO1 – Mickey's mother tries to restrict what he does, as she is clearly worried that he will turn into another Sammy.

Comment [JB(|: AO1 – The hatred that Mickey 'sometimes' has for Sammy lets the audience know that the two characters are very different from each

Comment [JB(|: AO3 – Although the 1960s were a time when economically the UK was not in recession, crime figures began to soar. Clearly, Sammy is

Comment [JB(|: AO2 – The 'toy car' robbery foreshadows the crime later in the play, when Mickey is sentenced to 'seven years' in prison for his part in the

Comment [JB(|: AO2 – The word 'bleedin'' is slang and identifies Mickey as a working-class child. Symbolically, it links with the title of the play and the idea that

Comment [JB(|: AO2 – 'Dead straight' is another example of slang from the north-west of England. Additionally, 'dead' foreshadows the end of Mickey's short

Comment [JB(|: AO2 – The double negative in his ungrammatical speech implies a lack of learning and educational opportunities

An' every time a hit.
He's allowed to play with matches,
And he goes to bed dead late,
And I have to go at seven,
Even though I'm nearly eight.
Y' know our Sammy,
He draws nudey women,
Without arms, or legs, or even heads
In the baths, when he goes swimmin'.
But I'm not allowed to go to the baths,
Me Mam says I have to wait,
'Cos I might get drowned, 'cos I'm only
seven,
But I'm not, I'm nearly eight.
Y' know our Sammy,
Y' know what he sometimes does?
He wees straight through the letter box
Of the house next door to us.
I tried to do it one night,
But I had to stand on a crate,
'Cos I couldn't reach the letter box
But I will by the time I'm eight.

Comment [JB(]: AO1 – Mickey's only ambition appears to be to emulate Sammy, who can 'spit', 'play with matches' and go 'to bed dead late'.

Comment [JB(]: AO1 – Mickey has an unhealthy admiration of Sammy, whose lack of humanity is revealed through his drawing. Sammy seems to be every inch a psychopath, who sees women sexually or 'nudey' but not as human beings.

Comment [JB(]: AO2 – The word 'drowned' is linked with death and although that is not how Mickey, it still foreshadows his fate somewhat.

Comment [JB(]: AO1 – Mickey wants to get away with misdemeanours like Sammy does. Inevitably, it will lead to becoming involved in more serious crimes.

Comment [JB(]: AO1 – It is true that by the time Mickey comes of age, he will increasingly fall into a life of crime. The audience, while laughing at the amusing aspects of the soliloquy, will find out later that Mickey will achieve his limited ambition of becoming more like Sammy. However, it will lead to his premature death.

AQA-style Specimen Assessment Material 17: Blood Brothers

How does Russell explore the theme of gender in *Blood Brothers*?

Write about:
• the ways particular characters change as they are affected by gender issues
• how Russell presents the theme of gender by the way he writes.

PLEASE NOTE, THERE ARE NO EXTRACTS FOR THE MODERN TEXTS SECTION, BUT THE FOLLOWING EXTRACT IS BELOW FOR GUIDANCE TO HELP YOU TO FORM AN ANSWER.

At this point in the play, Mrs Lyons has frantically been looking for Edward and is now panicking. This extract is important because the audience can see how even the comparatively powerful Mrs Lyons has to plead with her husband to get the move she wants.

EXTRACT

Mr Lyons *enters the garden.*

Mrs Lyons: Oh Richard, Richard.

Mr Lyons: For God's sake Jennifer, I told you on the phone, he'll just be out playing

Comment |JB(|: AO3 – Most families in the 1960s were more like the Lyonses than the Johnstones, in that the man was expected to go to work while the woman would stay at home.

Comment |JB(|: AO1 – Although Mr Lyons is not on stage much, he has a lot of power and influence, as is evidenced by Mrs Lyons crying out 'Oh Richard' upon seeing him.

Comment |JB(|: AO1 – Mr Lyons's impatience with his wife is obvious. He appears to think she should have more control over her domain, which is the domestic sphere.

somewhere.

Mrs Lyons: But where?

Mr Lyons: Outside somewhere, with friends. Edward…

Mrs Lyons: But I don't want him out playing.

Mr Lyons: Jennifer, he's not a baby. Edward…

Mrs Lyons: I don't care, I don't care…

Mr Lyons: For Christ's sake, you bring me home from work in the middle of the day, just to say you haven't seen him for an hour. Perhaps we should be talking about getting something for your nerves.

Mrs Lyons: There's nothing wrong with my nerves. It's just…just this place…I hate it. Richard, I don't want to stay here anymore. I want to move.

Mr Lyons: Jennifer! Jennifer, how many times…the factory is here, my work is

Comment [JB(]: AO1 – Mrs Lyons appears to be controlling, in that she wants to know exactly 'where' Edward is.

Comment [JB(]: AO1 – Mrs Lyons is quite clear about what she wants. She assertively says that she doesn't 'want' Edward 'out playing'. However, given Edward's age, it does seem to be an unreasonable demand.

Comment [JB(]: AO2 – Through the use of repetition and an ellipsis, the playwright shows how emotions are getting the better of Mrs Lyons.

Comment [JB(]: AO3 – Richard's reaction is stereotypical, as middle-class men in the 1960s would usually prioritise work over domestic issues.

Comment [JB(]: AO3 – Richard's reaction to this domestic crisis sums up the attitudes towards women's mental health that were prevalent before the 1960s, when it was quite common to lock wives up if they showed any signs of instability or even simply non-compliance.

Comment [JB(]: AO3 – Richard's dismissive attitude to what he considers to be stereotypically female problems (like 'nerves') is indicative of the thinly-disguised misogyny, which was more prevalent than now.

Comment [JB(]: AO2 – The use of repetition and ellipsis again emphasises how the strain of the situation is negatively affecting Mrs Lyons.
AO1 – She is not rationally explaining her reasons for moving but, later in the play, she gets her way anyway.

7

here…

Mrs Lyons: It doesn't have to be somewhere far away. But we have got to move, Richard. Because if we stay here I feel something terrible will happen, something bad.

Mr Lyons sighs and put his arm round Mrs Lyons.

Mr Lyons: Look, Jen. What is this thing you keep talking about getting away from? Mm?

Mrs Lyons: It's just…it's these people…these people that Edward has started mixing with. Can't you see how he's drawn to them? They're…they're drawing him away from me.

Mr Lyons, in despair, turns away from her.

Mr Lyons: Oh Christ.

He turns to look at her but she looks away. He sighs and absently bends to pick up a pair of children's shoes from the floor.

Comment [JB(]: AO2 – A rhetorical question shows how impatient the more rational Mr Lyons is becoming with his wife, who does not appear to be making sense.

Comment [JB(]: AO3 - Stereotypically, women have been more associated with feeling than men, who are thought to be more rational. Mrs Lyons is conforming to the stereotype with her almost hysterical behaviour.

Comment [JB(]: AO1 – Mr Lyons is condescending and patronising to his wife, who does not object to the way he treats her like a child,

Comment [JB(]: AO2 – The verb 'draw' could connote the violence of gunslingers that appear in Western movies, who wanted to be quick on the draw. If so, this foreshadows how Edward's short life is destined to end.

Comment [JB(]: AO1 – Mr Lyons's frustration with his wife is apparent here. There is a gulf of misunderstanding between him and the world of work he inhabits and the domestic sphere.

8

I really do think you should see a doctor.

> **Comment [JB(]:** AO1 – Mr Lyons does not specify what kind of doctor that his wife should see, but he is clearly questioning her mental stability.

AQA-style Specimen Assessment Material 18: Blood Brothers

How does Russell explore the theme of nature versus nurture in *Blood Brothers*?

Write about:
• how the theme of nature versus nurture is explored through characterisation
• how Russell presents the theme of nature versus nurture by the way he writes.

PLEASE NOTE, THERE ARE NO EXTRACTS FOR THE MODERN TEXTS SECTION, BUT THE FOLLOWING EXTRACT IS BELOW FOR GUIDANCE TO HELP YOU TO FORM AN ANSWER.

At this point in the play, Councillor Edward Lyons's public address has been interrupted by the gun-toting Mickey, who breaks the meeting up. This extract is important because the audience can see how different the two twins have become, despite being born to the same mother at the same time.

9

EXTRACT

Mickey *stops a couple of yards from* **Edward**. *He is unsteady and breathing awkwardly.*

Edward: *(eventually)* Hello, Mickey.

Mickey: I stopped takin' the pills.

Edward: *(pause)* Oh.

Mickey: *(eventually)* I began thinkin' again. Y' see. *(To the Councillor.)* Just get her out of here, mister, now!

The Councillors hurry off.

Edward *and* **Mickey** *are now alone* on the *platform.*

Mickey: I had to start thinkin' again. Because there was one thing left in my life. *(Pause.)* Just one thing I had left, Eddie – Linda – an' I wanted to keep her. So, so I stopped takin' the pills. But it was too late. D' y' know who told me about…you…an' Linda…Your mother…she came to the

10

Comment [JB(]: AO1 – Mickey is portray as 'unsteady', which is very unlike Eddie, his steady brother, whom has presided over a council meeting successfully until the untimely interruption. As a result of the way he has been nurtured, Eddie has risen to heights that Mickey could only ever dream about.

Comment [JB(]: AO1 – The stage direction makes the audience wonder why Edward is taking so long to respond to Mickey. It could be that he feels guilty about his 'light romance' with Linda or perhaps it is just fear. As an audience, we have to consider whether it was the way

Comment [JB(]: AO1 – Although working-class Mickey was not given 'pills' by his mother, he has been given them in prison to deal with his depression. Now that he has stopped taken them, he can see the situation more clearly and feels he has been taken advantage of by the

Comment [JB(]: AO2 – The cyclical structure of the plot is evident here, as like at their time of birth, the twins are together for this death scene. It gives the audience the possibility to make comparisons without the distractions of the other characters on stage.

Comment [JB(]: AO2 – Structurally, Russell uses a lot of pauses in this scene to heighten the drama and emphasise how Mickey has realised that nurture is more important than nature when it comes to determining one's fate in life.

Comment [JB(]: AO2 – The repetition of 'one thing' reminds the audience how desperate Mickey's situation is: he has been stripped of everything he holds dear, by virtue of his prison sentence, which was caused in turn by coming from a poor working-class single parent home.

Comment [JB(]: AO3 – As well as the 'pills' which were administered in prison and taken voluntarily by Mickey, he may have been given the chemical 'bromide' (mentioned by Mrs Johnstone earlier in the play) to suppress his sex drive. According to some reports, it was factory and told me.

Edward: Mickey, I don't know what she told you but Linda and I are just friends...

Mickey: *(shouting for the first time)* Friends! I could kill you. We were friends weren't we? Blood brothers, wasn't it? Remember?

Edward: Yes, Mickey, I remember.

Mickey: Well, how come you got everything...an' I got nothin'? *(Pause.)* Friends. I've been thinkin' again Eddie. You an' Linda were friends when she first got pregnant, weren't y'?

Edward: Mickey!

Mickey: Does my child belong to you as well as everythin' else? Does she, Eddie, does she?

Edward: *(shouting) No, for God's sake!*

Pause.

Comment [JB(]: AO3 – Despite all of the obstacles in his way, Mickey has managed to find work in a factory. Previously, we learned that the 'light romance' between Linda and Edward began while Mickey was working 'overtime'. Therefore, we could argue that hard work has only led to Mickey being exploited. This contradicts one of the fundamental principles of Thatcherism, which was that success came to those who chose to work hard.

Comment [JB(]: AO1 – Edward's response is deceitful, as the audience have already witnessed him kissing Mickey's wife and engaging in a 'light romance' with her. Perhaps, because of the way he was brought up, he may think this kind of behaviour and accompanying lie ('just friends') is acceptable.

Comment [JB(]: AO2 – The use of rhetorical question in this speech heaps doubt on the fairness of the system that sees Edward gain everything that he wants, while Mickey loses what little he has.

Comment [JB(]: AO1 – Now that Mickey has stopped taking pills, he thinks he can clearly see what has happened. His is no longer prepared to be passive and accepting of his fate, which seems predestined by his upbringing, and he wants answers.

Comment [JB(]: AO1 – The enormity of the class gap is beginning to sink in, as Mickey (in one of his rare lucid moments in Act 2) has realised that even his daughter may be Edward's. We suspect that Mickey may be paranoid, but nevertheless, it may be true.

11

From the back of the auditorium we hear a **Policeman** *through a loudhailer.*

Policeman 1: Now listen, son, listen to me; I've got armed marksmen with me. But if you do exactly as I say we won't need to use them, will we? Now look, Michael, put down the gun, just put down the gun, son.

Mickey: *(dismissing their presence)* What am I doin' here Eddie? I thought I was gonna shoot y'. But I can't even do that. I don't even know if the thing's loaded.

Mrs Johnstone slowly walks down the centre aisle towards the platform.

Policeman 2: What's that woman doin'?

Policeman 1: Get that woman away…

Policeman 2: Oh Christ.

Mrs Johnstone: Mickey. Mickey. Don't shoot him Mickey…

Mickey continues to hold the gun in position.

Comment [JB(]: AO2 – The name 'Michael' is symbolic of what could have been. Although Mickey must have been named Michael on his birth certificate, he has been brought up as Mickey. His life chance have been limited, in comparison to Edward, who is called 'Eddie' by working-class people but not by his parents.

Comment [JB(]: AO1 – Mickey's inability to do anything right could be a product of being brought up in a poor family that lacked aspirations. If Mickey had been imbued with self-confidence, his fate would have been very different.

Comment [JB(]: AO1 – The stage directions show us how resolute Mickey is, perhaps for the first time in his life. He is enraged by the injustice of the situation.

Mickey: Go away Mam…Mam you go away from here.

Mrs Johnstone: No, son. *(She walks on to the platform.)*

Mickey: *(shouting)* Mam!

Mrs Johnstone: Mickey. Don't shoot Eddie. He's your brother. You had a twin brother. I couldn't afford to keep both of you. His mother couldn't have kids. I agreed to give one of you away!

Mickey: *(something that begins deep down inside of him)* You! *(Screaming.)* You! Why didn't you give me away! *(He stands glaring at her, almost uncontrollable with rage.)* I could have been…I could have been him!

> **Comment [JB(]:** AO1 – Mrs Johnstone attemots to justify her decision by citing her financial reasons for parting with Edward. Ironically, we soon find out that Mickey wishes he had been given away instead.

> **Comment [JB(]:** AO1 – The injustice of the situation is too much for Mickey to bear. He wishes he had been randomly selected to enjoy an upbringing in a middle-class home instead of Edward.

> **Comment [JB(]:** AO2 – The anaphora of Mickey's last words make them resonate with the audience. The random selection of Edward over Mickey by Mrs Lyons has led to the twins experiencing very different lifestyles.

2 CONTEXT & TEXT SUMMARY

AO3: context

Although this AO is not as important as the first two AOs, it is still important to make a number of relevant comments depending on the question.

The time setting

The play is set between the 1960s and 1980s, which was an era when, arguably, when the class divide was more pronounced and obvious.

During the 1960s, 'youth culture' emerged as a force to be reckoned with. A pop group from Liverpool, called 'The Beatles', rose from a working class background to worldwide fame. Likewise, many young people began to aspire to be similarly upwardly mobile; they too wanted to go from 'rags to riches'. Many watched television and wanted to copy scenes from cowboy and gangster films and escape the humdrum of their daily lives.

Marilyn Monroe is mentioned numerous times in the play. She was a popular film star who died tragically at the age of 36 in 1962. The tragedy of a young death is explored through these references. Additionally, Monroe links to the theme of dreams, as many young women would have aspired to look like her. She was considered to be a 'dumb blonde' in the films she was cast in, which fitted into the dominant patriarchal society of that time. The woman in the nuclear family was expected to stay at home and look after the children, while the father went to work. Clearly, that is not the case with Mrs Johnstone, who has been deserted by her husband and been left to bring up her family by herself. Her position as a single mother would have been frowned upon in the 1960s and 1970s. Her predicament would have been worsened by the economic hardships faced by the working classes in the late 1970s and 1980s.

Even in 1982, when the play was first performed (without music), the Conservative Government were in power. The following year, (when music was added and 'Blood Brothers' took on its current form, the Prime Minister at the time, Margaret Thatcher, won a landslide victory. Her brand of politics, or economic liberalism, which involved controlling inflation rather than unemployment, made her extremely unpopular in the north, especially among the jobless. Clearly, this affected the playwright Willy Russell's view that he was 'brought up as a member of a class whose members were treated like second-class citizens'. This viewpoint may have been exacerbated by being the son of a former miner, when considering the animosity that was building up towards Thatcher, given the lack of government investment in the mining industry. Although Russell claims his father was 'not a party member or a tub-thumping socialist', he may have felt that the Conservatives were creating a huge divide in society. Additionally, the playwright understandably resented being treated as 'thick, daft, stupid and unworthy' based on what he perceived to be class prejudice. The play reflects Russell's belief that the class a person is born into dramatically affects their opportunities in life.

A year after 'Blood Brothers' became a musical, it was a miners' strike that threatened to bring down the Thatcher administration. It was unsuccessful. Russell himself observes the working classes inability to unite, when working at a warehouse: 'The foreman, himself a member of the working class, behaved like an animal because he had a little bit of power'. Perhaps the working classes are their own worse enemy, and this idea is explored in the play.

Although Mrs Thatcher is not directly mentioned in the play, her presence is felt through the economic suffering endured by the characters. During the 1980s, the country's unemployment figures soared well above the three million mark. Consequently, many jobless people had no option but to live 'on the dole'; their only income would be 'giro cheques' or government benefits. The only other option would be to turn to crime, like Sammy Johnstone in the play.

Due to the economic conditions, the divide between rich and poor was certainly more pronounced during the 1980s, as 'the haves and have-nots' led lives that were dramatically different, not unlike Edward and Mickey in the play. More cases of psychological depression and an increasing crime rate were unpleasant side effects of the economic recession.

The setting - places

Both Liverpool and Skelmersdale are areas where the Conservatives have traditionally struggled. However, the latter was a designated new town, where many Liverpudlians were expected to be rehoused away from the more cramped conditions of the city. Both middle and working classes live in each setting, not necessarily harmoniously, exemplified by the Lyons and the Johnstones respectively. The middle classes were relatively unaffected by the economic hardships of the 1980s, which increased working-class resentment.

2 THE PLAY

Act 1

Page 5

The play begins with Mrs Johnstone singing: 'Tell me it's not true'. The imperative used makes her appear as a strong woman.

The narrator acts like a Greek Chorus in that he informs the audience as to what is going on and is going to happen to the 'Johnstone twins'. He invites us to 'judge' for ourselves whether or not Mrs Johnstone has 'a stone in place of her heart'. This harsh metaphor reminds us how she is likely to be judged by others, but makes us ready to sympathise

The play begins at the end, as we see the twins dead on stage before Mrs Johnstone takes us back to the start. She mentions her smooth-talking husband: 'He said my eyes were deep pools, My skin as soft as snow'. This implies that she is a deep person, if we accept that eyes are the windows to the soul. The 'snow' is compared to her softness and it symbolises purity.

Already the audience can see that Mrs Johnstone was innocent when preyed upon by her husband, who says she is 'sexier than Marilyn Monroe'. We can see that time has taken its toll on her from the stage directions which describe her as 'aged thirty but looks more like fifty'. The comparison to Marilyn Monroe is the first of many, which shows the play's preoccupation with unrealised dreams. Many young women in the 60s longed to be considered as beautiful as Marilyn, but it all ended in tears as this film star died at the age of 35. The message in the motif is we can dream of glamour and perfection, but it ultimately unachievable.

Mrs Johnstone's coming of age (a thematic concern) and freedom is symbolised through 'dancing'. This feeling is quickly stripped away when she finds out that she is 'six weeks overdue' and grim reality threatens to ruin her life. However, 'at the registry' (rather than a church, which is arguably more romantic), she is still 'lovelier than Marilyn Monroe'.

Page 6

By the time she becomes pregnant for a second time, her husband will no longer take her 'dancing', as she is 'twice the size of Marilyn Monroe'. We, as an audience, feel sympathy for her, as her husband walks out on her 'with seven hungry mouths to feed and one more nearly due'. This use of synecdoche reminds us of how it's all about a single mother providing food for a growing family, as the children are shown as to us as nothing more than mouths with voracious appetites.

The drama increases as the milkman (played by the narrator) interrupts her with the milk bill, which she has to 'pay up today'. Milk makes us think of motherhood and conveys the idea that she is a responsible mother doing her best for her family. If she was providing them with fast food we'd have a completely different opinion about her.

Page 7
Nevertheless, Mrs Johnstone determinedly hangs onto her dreams. She hopes to get a job and thinks they'll 'live like kings'. We then see her with 'a brush, dusters and a mop bucket', which seems to indicate to us that she is an industrious, menial worker.

She is working at Mrs Lyons' house, and the first we see of the latter is when she enters with 'a parcel'. This implies that gifts come her way quite easily. Her concerns about her house being 'so big' makes us sympathise all the more with Mrs Johnstone, who is unlikely to have enough room for her huge family.

Page 8
The contrast continues as we discover that Mrs Lyons cannot have babies, when she says: 'we thought children would come along'. We have some sympathy with Mrs Lyons, at this point.

Mrs Johnstone replies that: 'Havin' babies, it's like clockwork to me'. This reminds subtly of her working-class roots, as giving birth is like clocking in and out and working in a factory.

Emphasising the idea that Mrs Johnstone is walked over in life, as a female member of the underclass, is Mrs Lyons' actions: putting 'a pair of new shoes' onto the table. Additionally, this is when we discover that Mrs Johnstone is superstitious. The narrator adds his comment that 'there's one lone magpie overhead', a bird which traditionally symbolises bad luck.

Page 9
The narrator turns from milkman to gynaecologist, as he reveals that Mrs Johnstone is 'expecting twins'. Given her financial predicament, this is terrible news for her as 'the Welfare have already been on to' her. There is the danger that her children could be put 'into care'. Nevertheless, she loves 'the bones of every one of them'. This figure of speech links to death, as we can picture her children as skeletons rather than flesh and blood. We also get the impression that the government agencies are unsympathetic, with her negative comment about the Welfare State.

Page 10
The threat of 'the Welfare' is what allows Mrs Lyons' 'idea' of taking one of the twins to grow 'as surely as a seed, in a mother's womb'. The positive simile makes the idea seem quite palatable, especially as it is voiced by the seemingly neutral narrator.

Page 11

The idea of her child living 'in a palace' has a certain, understandable appeal to Mrs Johnstone. This metaphor reminds us that, in comparison, Mrs Johnstone must be living in squalor.

Page 12

Mrs Lyons is determined to make sure the plan reaches fruition, as as 'suddenly reaches for the Bible' to make their deal 'a binding agreement'.

Page 13

The narrator remarks that: 'In the name of Jesus [...] there's a deal been born'. This reminds us that both women have sworn on the Bible, and cannot change their minds without serious repercussions.

Once he exits, the catalogue man and the finance man harass Mrs Johnstone for payments, which reminds us how much she is struggling financially.

Page 14

Eventually, Mrs Johnstone concludes that 'nothing's yours'. She realises that she has been seduced by dreams, sold by the catalogue which makes expensive goods appear affordable when it is broken down into weekly payments and 'there's six months to pay'.

Page 15

She continues to sing about 'living on the never never', which reminds us that she is unlikely to escape the poverty trap she lives in. On that note, Mrs Lyons enters and demands the baby, although Mrs Johnstone requests to 'keep them for a few more days'.

Page 16

After having given up her baby, Mrs Johnstone has to lie to her children. She tells them that Mickey's twin has 'gone up to heaven'. In a sense, this works as a metaphor, for her child is living with Mrs Lyons', whose house is palatial compared to hers.

Page 17

For the first time, we hear from Mr Lyons, who says how 'proud' he is of Edward, (the baby that Mrs Johnstone has given rather than sold to Mrs Lyons) and his wife, Jennifer, who has not actually given birth to a child. This shows how detached Mr Lyons is from parenting, as he does not seem to suspect his wife, at all.

We are reminded that class warfare is never far away from this play, as Mrs Lyons reveals her concern about Mrs Johnstone 'cuddling' Edward 'as if she were his mother'. Prior to that, she expresses her opinion to her husband that 'babies catch things very easily, Richard'. This shows that she views he working class as almost parasite infested and she is desperate to keep her distance from them. The irony is she has a son who has a working-class bloodline. It seems to indicate that she believes in the importance of environmental factors over genetics when it comes to a child's upbringing.

Page 18

We discover that Mrs Lyons is ready to deceive her husband again as she asks for 'about fifty pounds', which she claims is 'for the baby' and 'the nursery'. We later discover that she intends to use it to pay off Mrs Johnstone and keep her silent. Given the extent of her deceit, she has a lot of nerve to threaten Mrs Johnstone, by saying: 'You gave your baby away. Don't you realise what a crime that is'.

Page 19

Mrs Lyons continues to manipulate Mrs Johnstone by exploiting her superstitious fears 'about twins, secretly parted', when the former says: 'You won't tell anyone about this [...] because if you do, you will kill them [the twins]'. A terrified Mrs Johnstone does not throw the money away when Mrs Lyons puts it into her hands for a second time, perhaps as she resigned to her fate: she must stay quiet to save the twins' lives.

Page 20

Foreshadowing the finale of the play, we see Mickey 'carrying a toy gun'. We feel sympathy for him for he complains about his brother, Sammy, who has 'robbed' him of his 'best gun'.

Page 21

We see how being a working-class child can result in Mickey becoming 'desultory' or lacking in purpose. He cannot entertain himself, and sits 'bored', complaining about Sammy, who has 'robbed' him of his 'toy car'.

Page 22

Mickey's life changes for the better upon meeting Edward, who generously 'offers' him a sweet, although he has to be prompted first.

Page 23

Mickey uses the slang word 'dead' as an intensifier to describe how 'careful' you have to be if Sammy 'gives y' a sweet'. Edward uses the word 'smashing' to describe Mickey's swearing and sometimes vulgar vocabulary. The word 'smashing' implies violence, which is prevalent in the text. We find out that Sammy has 'a plate in his head', which makes us sympathise with him a little, as it partly explains his behaviour.

Page 24

The plate in Sammy's head is used for comic effect when Mickey speculates that it must be 'one of them little plates that you eat bread off'.

After finding out they share the same birthday, Mickey asks Edward if he wants to become his 'blood brother'. Even this process involves violence and a 'penknife', although Mickey warns 'it hurts'.

Page 25

Sammy appears and claims that he is going to 'get an air gun'. From this statement, we can see that violent playing is going to escalate into 'real' violence.

Page 26

Sammy himself appears to an omen of doom, for he claims that his worms are 'dead' now, although they were alive in the morning.

Page 27

Even Mrs Johnstone seems threatening to Edward, as she warns him of the 'bogey man'. Nevertheless, we can understand the reasoning behind her scaring Edward away.

When Edward gets home, we realise his father has little time for him. Mr Lyons promises if the 'merger' is completed then 'the firm will run itself' and he'll have 'plenty of time' to spend with his family. Edward's father is only slightly less absent than Mickey's.

Page 28

The juxtaposition of education against superstition is highlighted by Edward asking his father: 'Daddy, how do you spell bogey man?' Clearly, Edward wants to use a dictionary to improve his knowledge. Mrs Lyons adds that it is the sort of term that 'a silly mother might' use. This adds to the idea that Edward is receiving a better upbringing than Mickey, who only has his loving but superstitious mother to guide him through life.

Page 29

By contrast, Mrs Lyons is over-protective of Edward, and tells him she does not want him 'mixing' with boys like Mickey. After hearing him swear, she is worried he will 'learn filth from them'.

Page 30

We now meet another significant female character as Linda stands out in the gang as more intelligent than the rest of the children. Although Sammy says he's 'shot' her and Mickey with a toy gun, she says she 'stopped it with the bin lid'. This implies that although she is surrounded by rubbish, she is able to fight the inevitable, which for the twins is a premature death.

Page 31

The children continue to play increasingly violent games, as they become 'a brigade of US troops'. Once again, Linda stands out from the crowd, as she 'lobs' the grenade back where it came from. It seems as if she is indestructible.

Page 32

We also discover that Linda is ready prepared to protect Mickey from the rest of the children and is even brave enough to threaten Sammy with her 'mother' if he does not 'leave him alone!' Using the imperative makes her appear stronger than the other characters.

Page 33

The misogynistic society is revealed when Mickey introduces Linda to Edward, by saying: 'She's a girl but she's all right'. She clearly is the strongest, as she is portrayed producing 'the air pistol' and she is the one who tells them that 'Peter Pan' is the target. This implies that 'Peter Pan', the fictional character who wants to stay young forever is the enemy. They need to grow up and learn, although there is a certain amount of irony as the twins, like Peter Pan will never grow old.

Page 34

Although the children are having fun, the narrator reminds us how this will change as 'the devil's got' their 'number'. This is refrain that repeats and here the mood switches from jovial to sombre very quickly.

Page 35

Superstition dominates as Mrs Lyons 'sweeps' her husband's 'shoes' off the table, echoing what happened earlier in the play. It appears that she is now as superstitious as Mrs Johnstone. She insists that they move.

Page 36

When we return to the children, we witness that Linda is 'not scared' of throwing 'some stones through them windows'. However, she notes that 'Eddie's scared'. Mickey defends his blood brother, by saying: 'No, he isn't!'

Page 37

However, Linda has highlighted how different Edward is. Now he makes the audience realise how much he does not fit in with working-class children, as he misinterprets Linda and Mickey's 'terrified glances', 'mistaking their look for encouragement'. Linda disowns him, saying to the policeman: 'He's not with us'.

Page 38

The policeman takes Edward back to Mrs Lyons and tries to downplay the criminal activity as 'more of a prank'. This shows class discrimination, as the policeman would be unlikely to adopt the same tone, if addressing Mrs Johnstone.

The plot is driven by the 'prank', which convinces Mr Lyons to move 'further out towards the country'.

Page 39

Edward is beside himself with grief at the thought of moving and decides to say goodbye to Mrs Johnstone and Mickey. Edward cries and she cradles him, saying: 'Don't you be soft'. She sees the irony in the situation as she says: 'Here's you wantin' to stay here, an' here's me, I've been tryin' to get out'.

Page 40

When Edward and his family move, he notices 'a magpie'. He knows the superstition that 'it's one [magpie] for sorrow' and tells his mother. Mrs Lyons dismisses it as 'stupid', which ironic given her new-found belief about shoes on the table bringing bad luck.

Page 41

Now that Mickey is without his blood brother, he sings about 'killing time'. This figure of speech reminds us that he will be killed later in the play. Mickey misses Edward who is 'clean, neat and tidy'.

Page 42

Edward misses Mickey who can 'swear like a soldier', and soon both are singing in unison: 'My friend'.

The mood quickly changes as Mrs Johnstone sings about 'movin' away'. The personification of her 'reputation' which is 'following' her makes us realise how the past affects the future.

Page 43

Mrs Johnstone seems naive enough to believe that in Skelmersdale 'the air is so pure, / You can get drunk just by breathing'. It appears that she is still a dreamer.

Page 44

She now appears to relishing the opportunity to go 'dancing' again. She appears to be a Catholic as she imagines 'His Holiness' flying in 'from Rome'. Her religious belief makes the vow she took earlier in the play all the more difficult to break.

Page 45

Mrs Johnstone ends Act 1 with the words: 'bright new day'. She is clearly looking forward to a new start.

Act Two

Page 46

Mrs Johnstone begins by telling the audience how 'lovely' the new house is, although the neighbours 'sometimes fight on Saturday night'. This makes us think that Skelmersdale is not so different from Liverpool and the rough life she was accustomed to.

However, she has found romance in Joe, the milkman, who 'sometimes' takes her 'dancing'. Nevertheless, she is burdened by Sammy being on 'probation', after burning 'the school down'.

Page 47

We hear that Mickey is 'secret dancing', which shortly afterwards we see Edward dancing with his mother, Mrs Lyons, who is deeply insecure. Even Edward wonders what she is 'on about', when she says: 'we're safe here, aren't we?' The repetition of question tags adds to the idea that she is need of reassurance.

Page 48

Mrs Johnstone is also worried, as is she 'hustling Mickey to school'. She is concerned that he's going to be 'late'.

Page 49

The narrator, who has reappeared as a bus conductor, reminds Mrs Johnstone that 'no one gets off without the price being paid'. It seems to suggest that the past will catch up with her.

Sammy, later, confronts the conductor with a 'knife'.

Page 50

Another confrontation follows, as Edward is ordered to hand over the 'locket' that Mrs Johnstone had given him earlier to his teacher.

Page 51

Edward stoically accepts his fate, which is to be 'suspended' from school. Meanwhile, Mickey is subjected to taunts from his teacher, who asks: 'how the hell do you hope to get a job when you never listen to anythin' ?' This rhetorical question emphasises how powerful messages are from teachers, who have the capacity to reduce students' self-esteem.

Page 52

Nevertheless, Mickey is undaunted, as he sarcastically replies: 'Yeh an' it'll really help me to get a job if I know what some soddin' pygmies in Africa have for their dinner'. Ironically, he may not realise his ignorance, as his teacher was asking him about a different continent: 'the Boro Indian of the Amazon Basin'.

Page 53

Meanwhile, the locket continues to cause Edward problems, as his mother asks about the photograph: 'When were you photographed with that woman'. Of course, she does not know it is his twin brother, Mickey, who appears in the picture.

Page 54

After some more prophetic words of doom and gloom from the narrator, Linda tries to make Mickey more passionate. She even attempts to make him jealous: 'he's [that lad lookin' out the window] gorgeous'.

Page 55

Meanwhile, Edward reveals how much he admires his blood brother, whose 'hair's dark and wavy', while his is 'mousey to fair'. The word 'mousey' reminds us that Edward is meek and mild compared to his brother, who represents his 'dark' side.

Page 56

Nevertheless, Mickey needs Edward's help when it comes to Linda, as 'the words just disappear'. By contrast, Edward's education has given him a mastery over language that makes it easy for him to advise his brother.

Page 57

The closer Edward gets to Mickey, the more distant he gets from his mother, whom he describes as 'off her beam'. This could be considered as light imagery, but it is used in a negative way. Mrs Lyons is following the boys, while the narrator asks her a rhetorical question: 'Did you really feel that you'd become secure'?

Page 58

Meanwhile, when Mrs Johnstone asks the boys what film they are going to see at the cinema, they both have different replies. Edward's answer 'Dr Zhivago' is more romantic than Mickey's more violent 'Magnificent Seven' reply.

Page 59

Strangely, like Edward, Mickey questions his mother's sanity, calling her a 'head case'. We realise that the two mothers have more in common than they would like to admit, so it is less surprising when they meet.

Page 60

Once again, Mrs Lyons attempts to buy off Mrs Johnstone, this time with 'thousands'. The latter is realistic enough to realise that she would just 'buy more junk and trash' with the money.

Page 61

Meanwhile, Edward and Mickey are experiencing the same 'ecstatic agony' after their cinematic experience. Edward shows his class again by wondering if Wimbledon will 'ever be the same'. Tennis is a sport traditionally associated with the rich.

Page 62

The differences between the twins is exemplified by Mickey lying to Linda, by telling her they'd just seen 'Bridge Over The River Kwai'. By contrast, Edward is about to tell her the truth.

Page 63

The narrator moves the plot through the space of three years, as he doubles up as 'the rifle range man at the fairground'. He seems to represent the inescapable nature of fate or destiny. The hidden message appears to be to ignorance is bliss, as he says: 'who'd tell the lambs in Spring' that they will be slaughtered in a different season.

Page 64

The narrator repeats the triplet, using direct address: 'When you're young, free and innocent and just eighteen'. This emphasises how tragic it is for someone that age to lose their life, as we've seen Linda and the twins enjoying their lives at the fair.

Linda appears flirtatious, in a joking way at least, as she says to Edward, when they are alone: 'looking for a good time? Ten to seven.'

Page 65

Edward flirts in return, telling Linda that he 'would have asked' her to marry him 'years ago', if he were Mickey. He sings and attempts to use poetry to win her heart, although he says he'd only say it if he 'could stand inside his shoes'. He's been hypocritical because he says he's 'not saying a word', but he's actually recited a line from Shakespeare's Sonnet 18: Shall 'I compare thee to a summer's day'.

Page 66

Mickey interrupts, after working 'overtime' and his generosity is in evidence as he tells Edward that 'the Christmas party's gonna be on' him.

Page 67

That same generous nature is seen in his mother, as Mrs Johnstone 'nods' when he asks if his pregnant wife-to-be, Linda, can live with them 'for a bit'.

Page 68

Mrs Johnstone doubles up as Miss Jones, a secretary, as she types a few letters dictated by her boss, Mr Lyons. The political message is that business is heartless, as it is all about profits rather than people, with Mr Lyons blaming 'the shrinking pound' among other economic factors for the letter of dismissal.

Page 69

Eventually, Miss Jones is typing a letter of dismissal to herself, which states without feeling: 'we'd like to thank you / Many years of splendid service, / Etcetera blah blah blah'. This shows how little her contribution is valued.

Page 70

We soon discover that Mickey has lost his job, which he 'hated', that involved 'standin' there all day never doin' nothin' but put cardboard boxes together'. It sounds menial and meaningless, but it's all he had and now it's gone.

Page 71

Edward is out of touch with Mickey's reality, as he says if he were him he'd 'draw the dole' and 'live like a bohemian'. Mickey ends up threatening Edward, whom he describes as 'a kid'. By contrast, Mickey has grown up the hard way.

Page 72

Two scenes run simultaneously as Sammy puts pressure on Mickey to earn 'fifty quid', by helping him commit a crime. This is the same sum that was offered by Mrs Lyons to Mrs Johnstone for his silence. It connects the two activities, showing that selling a child is also just as criminal. The motivation for Mickey is the fact he has 'nothing' and won't be able to take his 'tart' anywhere for 'New Year', as Sammy puts it. The word 'tart' shows how dismissive he is about female, seeing them only a sex objects, as the word 'tart' can mean 'prostitute'.

Ironically, while Mickey is being tempted by money, Linda is being tempted by Edward, who confesses that he 'always loved' her. She replies that she has 'always...loved' him, 'in a way'. This hesitation seems to indicate confusion, on her part and prompts Edward to use the imperative: 'Then marry me.' The absence of an exclamation mark makes it a little less demanding, but he is still being relatively forceful with his brother's wife, not to mention disloyal.

Page 73

Mickey, meanwhile, expecting to financially benefit from his involvement in Sammy's criminal activity, tells Linda they're going out 'dancin''. This motif links to the characters' dreams of a life of glamour, which is unachievable to the working-class characters.

Even the crime affects working-class people, as the narrator informs us that 'there's a man lying bleeding on a garage floor' after Sammy uses his gun. This reminds us that the working-class lack unity and fight between themselves, as garage-work is associated with that socio-economic group.

Page 74

Mrs Johnstone acts as a narrator and relates as she sings that the seven-year jail sentence has left Mickey 'off the rails, / Just like Marilyn Monroe / His mind's gone dancing'. For the first time, 'dancing' is used to mean insanity.

Page 75

We soon realise that Mickey is now dependent on anti-depressant tablets, which he thinks he needs to take 'cos they make' him 'better'. This shows how naive and controlled by his environment he is. He lacks the education to make an independent decision to rid himself of the dependency.

His mother, continuing the role of narrator, which makes us feel more sympathy for his plight, tells us that Mickey's 'speech is rather slow' and 'you'd think he was dead'. This foreshadows what is about to happen.

We suspect that Linda has possibly been up to some skullduggery of her own, when she's asked by her mother-in-law about the new place she's got for herself, Mickey and their child. She says 'he's on the housin' committee'. We may wonder who it is and what her relationship is with this character.

Page 77

Mickey soon reveals that 'a job and a house' has been 'sorted out' by her and 'Councillor Eddie Lyons'. His pride is hurt, which makes him want to 'be invisible'. Therefore, he takes his 'tablets'.

The narrator describes how the 'girl inside the woman' wants to 'get free'. This description adds a touch of innocence to the 'light romance' (to use Mrs Johnstone's description) that follows with Eddie, which she initiates.

Page 78

After we see them 'kiss', Mrs Johnstone describes them as 'just two fools', who 'break' the rules. Mrs Johnstone seems to have learned from bitter experience that they are 'gonna have to pay' for their indiscretions.

Page 79

While Mrs Johnstone continues her song, Mrs Lyons is informing Mickey of the situation: pointing out 'Edward and Linda to him'.

As Mickey retrieves Sammy's gun from under the floorboards, the narrator reveals that 'there's a man gone mad'. We expect that Mickey will shoot either one or both of the secret lovers.

Page 80

Meanwhile, Edward is busy 'addressing his audience' at the Town Hall. Ironically, on another matter entirely, he says: 'there is a light at the end of the tunnel'. We know the darkness of death awaits him, although Mickey has seen the light of what his wife and blood brother are doing, as he reveals with a gun in his hand that: 'I stopped takin' the pills'. He is no longer prepared to be exploited.

Page 81

Now he is not on medication, Mickey's suspicions are aroused, as he says: 'You an' Linda were friends when she first got pregnant'. Clearly, he thinks that Edward's affair is more than a 'light romance' and it makes him question who is the father of his child.

As the police and Mrs Johnstone arrive, trying to placate Mickey, his mother reveals: 'He's your twin brother'.

Page 82

Rather than pacifying him, the revelation infuriates Mickey, who says: 'I could have been him!' Perhaps overcome with anger and other emotions, the gun accidentally goes off, blowing 'Edward apart'. Consequently, the police blow 'Mickey away'.

The narrator asks us if we should blame 'superstition' or 'class' for 'what came to pass'. The rhyme persuasively suggests that we should choose the latter explanation.

Page 83

The play's finale involves the whole company repeating: 'Tell me it's not true'. They want to believe that 'it's just pretend' and 'just the end [...] / Of an old movie with Marilyn Monroe'. Of course, her life ended prematurely when she committed suicide in August 1962. Like Mickey, she suffered from depression and it ended in tragedy.

Printed in Great Britain
by Amazon